# Moving Forward

Also by Bruce Bruinsma

*Live with Meaning*

# MOVING FORWARD

Putting Your Future Funded Ministry Into Motion

BRUCE BRUINSMA

Print Edition

BruceBruinsma.com

# CONTENTS

# Introduction

Christians are all called to ministry for a lifetime. Impacting and changing lives is more than a priority. It is God's mandate to each of us. We understand that this mandate; this call on our lives can be viewed in two ways.

First, there is a common call, the mandate that as Chris- tians we are all ministers and are all called to impact others and help change lives. And second, there is a unique call, an invitation to walk into our preferred future. This call is a uniquely personal one, and we understand it each in our own way.

An important point is this: our unique call defines our Kingdom purpose and points us to our preferred future. Remember the boy, Samuel? His response to God was, "Speak, for your servant is listening."

When we speak of the Kingdom, we refer to the heart of Jesus' teachings, which center around the theme of the Kingdom of God. This Kingdom includes how we internalize Jesus' teachings and life directions as well as how we represent Him to the world. He challenges us to be both the light to the world and the yeast in it. So, our "individual Kingdom purpose" reflects God's call on our lives and how we respond to that call. That call is our unique Kingdom purpose—yes, our preferred future.

The below quote and verse will help you focus on your future:

*Retirement is not only a reward for past service, it is a stepping stone to future ministry.*
Bruce Bruinsma

*If we live, we live for the Lord; and if we die, we die for the Lord. So, whether we live or die, we belong to the Lord.*
Romans 14:8 (NIV)

My hope is that you connect and engage with this important message. Without personal vision, relevant preparation, and a sustainable financial plan, you cannot serve faithfully for a lifetime. The lack of preparation gets in the way. Often God is preparing you without you even being aware it is happening. By the time you see the pattern of preparation clearly, the preparation is already complete. This is one of the ways we are blessed by God.

Funding your future ministry is another key element of your preparation. It is the preparation giving us the freedom to serve. "Future Funded Ministry" is the name first given by Envoy Financial to describe the financial preparation for your lifetime of service.

In my first book on the subject of Future Funded Ministry, Finding Freedom, Understanding the Power of Future Funded Ministry, I outlined a four-part journey. That journey was designed to help you understand what Future Funded Ministry is about and why it is important. It introduced the paramount and powerful concept of living life with purpose and meaning.

I introduced these six important insights:

1. The myth of retirement, with its focus on "do-ing nothing" or only satisfying our personal

desires, stems from an entirely secular point of view.

2. The realization that we now live longer.

3. The deep understanding of what it means to impact lives in the name of Jesus. This starts with a common call to ministry and then grows out of a unique, personal, and individual understanding of God's call on your life.

4. The results of poor planning—life without a Future Funded Ministry Plan.

5. The success stories and how lives are impacted—we introduced you to a few of our Future Funded Ministry Champions.

6. The DNA of meaning or living life with purpose, this is the heart of our message.

If you have not read the prior book, it will be helpful to do so. You can download it for FREE at BruceBruinsma.com

# 1

## A Practical Guide To Putting Your Future into Motion, and Doing It Now!

### The DNA of Meaning

So, let's begin this book with where we left off in the prior one—to remind you that how you respond to the challenges of life shape how you think. It is your life experiences that define who you are and impact the future choices you make. The ones that impact you the most, the ones that stick with you and shape you, are the ones that elicit the most emotional connection and the greatest impact.

When you are emotionally connected and fully engaged in the experience, something that is even more powerful when others are involved, it makes the deepest impression. By interfacing with others in the activities of daily living, you understand at  a deep level how and where you live as a Jesus follower and witness for him.

The moments of engagement and introspection, while becoming an "all in" participant in the key events of your life, help you capture and retain those pivotal moments embraced by the term, DNA of Meaning. By saving and savoring those moments, they inspire the deepest memories of your life.

These are the relationships or connections that mold and shape our lives. This is the DNA of Meaning, the collection of deep emotional connections that create a life of meaning and purpose deep within us. God seeds our lives with natural DNA plus spiritual gifts and emotional experiences, creating the way for us to prepare and discover our pathway to a life of meaning for and with Him. God both calls us and prepares us for future ministry—ministry that can flourish in every stage of life, culminating with the 4th Quarter and the three stages that compose it. How does the DNA of meaning play out in our lives? Our powerful emotional moments are strung together and leave an indelible imprint that guides our responses and decisions. A powerful and God directed force is created when the results of our experience are coupled with His direction. Through those connections, you discover your higher purpose in life and your specific role in building God's Kingdom in each and every stage of life.

A life without purpose is a life without meaning. A life without meaning is a life without hope. And a life without hope results in distancing you from God and certainly His plan for your life.

**Your Top Priority**

Your top priority in life, after knowing God and making Him number one, is to explore and discover your life's purpose and how you can best serve Him. When you internalize your role in building God's kingdom you will experience the impact of what it means to be faithful for a lifetime and the priority of having a Future Funded Ministry in place. You will then capture the most meaningful and deepest desires of your heart.

Understand that when I say "life," I mean life to the

end of it, not just until an arbitrary time of "retirement." Most of us are living longer; therefore, odds are that you will live longer too. My desire is that your actions produce both satisfaction and eternal significance for a lifetime. God's plan for you, your meaning and purpose, is what will drive you when you discover it. This emotional engine will bring energy and focus until the very end.

## Take Responsibility

In addition to connecting with and understanding your God directed purpose, there is one more necessary action step. You have to take responsibility for the financial part of the plan and actually fund your future ministry. You must start funding it now in order to fulfill and serve your purpose until the very end of life.

Serving Jesus with both purpose and adequate funding fully prepares you to live out an extended and meaningful life. Your life will be evidenced by confidence and joy; the joy of being in a fulfilling relationship with God even when times are tough. His promise to uphold you during trying times makes the difference between failure and success. It is the margin when needed the most. It is the difference between falling forward or falling backward.

**Now What? How Do I Fund the Future?**

As a result of understanding the principles outlined above, you ask yourself, "What can I do now to not just understand my calling and future ministry, but understand how I can actually fund my calling and future ministry? Where do I start?" Or, if started, "How do I successfully finish?" You ask yourself, "Am I too late?" or even, "Isn't it too early?" There are so many questions: "What do I do with my 401(k), 403(b), or 403(b)(9)? My IRA? My pension? Social Security? What is the best way to start? How do I even approach planning? What does investing look like?"

The questions are never ending—they are not simply confusing, but they can be scary and often over-whelming. This book is here to help.

Moving Forward is dedicated to answering those questions and many more of the nagging variety. It is focused on providing a clear context for your explo-ration and journey towards understanding. The goal here is to make you more comfortable and confident during your journey while increasing your productivity when serving God. There is freedom and joy when you are financially equipped to undertake your mission and contribute to building His earthly kingdom. How great it is to be firmly in His will, comfortable, not dependent on others monetarily, and to be financially stress free? Great indeed!

**Acknowledge This Truth: A Personal Prayer to be Prayed Now**

*I openly acknowledge God's capacity to care for me in all circumstances and have faith that He will provide the resources to carry out His plan for my life. However, I also believe that He challenges me to be prepared and to steward the time, talent, and resources He puts at my disposal for His glory.*

**My Future Vision Statement:**

My Vision for the Future:

_____

_____

_____

My Reason for Moving Forward:

_____

_____

_____

My Current Financial Landscape:

_____

_____

_____

My Desired Financial Landscape in 5 Years, 10 Years, 25 Years, and Retirement:

_____

_____

_____

_____

_____

**My Preparation for Implementation:**
God's Prepared Future for Me

Financial:

_____

_____

With My Spouse:

_____

_____

Spiritual:

_____

_____

Other:

_____

_____

I'm committed to moving forward.
**The next step I'm going to take is:**
Increase Savings: _____

Get out of Debt: _____

Increase Income: _____

Signature: _____

# 2

## Putting Your Future Funding into Motion

It is now time to learn how to put Future Funded Ministry into motion—to take it out of neutral and put it into gear. It is time to both understand and design the practical steps by which you can create a Future Funded Ministry strategy and a "Motion Plan." With a plan in place, you can be confident in building your meaningful, rich, and God-honoring retirement. You will have a stress-free, independent time of future ministry. Future Funded Ministry will empower your life, change your life, and you can start today!

## Background and Foundation

Before we continue, I want you to be encouraged. It is never too early nor too late to move towards your future and to put your plan—your financial plan, your stewardship plan, your money plan—into motion. If you are on the back end of middle age, you can still fully fund your future ministry.

If you are in your twenties or thirties, it is not too early to start. The best idea is to start as early as possible. We will take your age into account when you begin the planning process. You can take steps today to improve your future regardless of your age or life stage. Not only that, it does not matter how much money or how many assets you have or think you have. In other words, now is the key strategic and tactical time to begin or improve your financial preparation leading to ministry for a lifetime.

## Let's Get Started

We begin from where you are right now, whether you have started or not. The important step is to put a plan into motion. You have both your common and kingdom purpose to carry out. You will carry it out during what the world calls "retirement." We now understand that there are three stages during this 4th Quarter.

Yes, three stages that make up those years between 65 and 95. Those stages roughly encompass ages 67-78, 79-87, and 88 on—what we call early retirement, middle retirement, and late retirement.

The important thing, and thus the focus of this book, is to start planning now so that you can picture a future where money does not get in the way of retirement and God's call on your life.

**Some Goals**

As we uncovered in book 1, *Finding Freedom, Understanding the Power of Future Funded Ministry*, there are some universal goals for you. You are challenged to hit these goals during retirement, and depending on your age when you read this, perhaps in your current retirement life stage:

- Continue to serve the Lord faithfully.

- Seamlessly support your family.

- Remain independent, not dependent, upon family, children or government.

- Complete the items on your bucket list.

- Live comfortably, happily, and purposefully with love and compassion.

- Find freedom while focusing on your own personal ministry and the ministry you share with others, your community, and your church.

During that first stage, ages 67-78—early retirement, there will be a lot of action. During the second stage, ages 79-87—middle retirement, leadership through mentoring and sharing are the priorities. And during the third stage (88+)—later retirement, valuable reflection and experienced based insights enhanced through meaningful sharing becomes your role. The final act of the final stage is certainly death. A grand entrance into eternity. Be faithful. Be encouraged.

3

# The Three Stages of Retirement

When people, even analysts, talk about retirement they talk about it as being one homogeneous season of life. They generally characterize it as a time of retreat and diminished capacity. Nothing could be further from the truth and further than the meaning of retirement from God's perspective.

There are limitations to our understanding about retirement because of a lack of knowledge about and experience with the three stages of the 4th Quarter. In addition to those limitations, we each have our individual capacity and capabilities, including the associated limitations. Our unique limitations reduce our capacity to make a difference in every season of life, including the 4th Quarter. While all seasons are important, the 4th Quarter of life is important because so little is known or written about it. It is one of the great opportunities of our time to build an ever-expanding cadre of dedicated, world-changing Christians. The Christian Management Association of Australia recently launched a new ministry completely focused on the Christian's calling in the 4th Quarter. This is clearly a worldwide issue with Kingdom opportunity written all over it. HBO even released a documentary (written, directed, and acted by those 90 or over) entitled, "If Your Name is Not in The Obits, Eat Breakfast." Seems like a good plan to me.

Our generalized, and often wrong perception about the 4th Quarter, is rooted in the historical timeline of longevity. In 1936, when Social Security was introduced, our life expectancy in the United States was 63. Today, it is closer to 85 or 90, and for those born in 2010, life expectancy is projected to be upwards of 104. Because there is an expanded period of time for the last season of life, there is room for new and important roles for us to play. Now is the time to identify those new stages of life, those important new roles, and to manage our expectations.

It is also time for Christians to realize the new and expanded roles we can play in building the Kingdom of God here on earth. We can make vital contributions to Kingdom expansion during each of those seasons and life stages. It is reasonable to confirm that just as there are roles in the Kingdom during our earlier stages of life, there are valuable roles during the last seasons. As a 75-year-old opined, "God must not be done with me yet because here I stand."

## The Three Stages of Retirement in Detail

If there can be meaning and purpose for our lives during the early stages of retirement, why not during the later stages as well? Those stages are as distinct as the stages bounded by ages 30-40, 40-50, or 50-60. Each stage has unique and identifiable characteristics. Each stage can be filled with meaning and purpose connected to God's plan for your whole life. Yes, there is a River of Life that flows from the Throne of God through you.

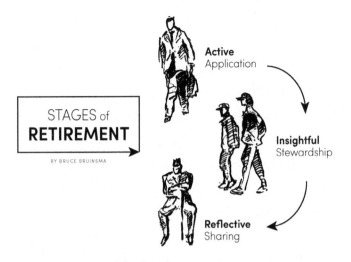

STAGES of
**RETIREMENT**

BY BRUCE BRUINSMA

**Active**
Application

**Insightful**
Stewardship

**Reflective**
Sharing

Here is a quick overview of the three stages of retirement. This is the beginning of a new way for us to think about, understand, and put in motion our Future Funded Ministry.

# Active
## Application

**Active Application (age 67 -78)**

Early Retirement: The ability and capacity to put into practice what you have learned up to this point in your life. You can lead, be very productive, and bring energy to all your endeavors.

***Problems and Questions:***
What do I do with my time?
Do we move or stay where we are?
How do I manage my money and expenses?
Does anybody value my experience and knowledge?

**Insightful Stewardship (age 79-87)**

Middle Retirement: The ability and energy to bring wisdom and insight to any opportunity or situation through mentoring. Leadership roles will be collaborative and marked by the ability to bring perspective, support, and encouragement to those who will lead in the future. You will bring value to any discussion or decision.

You will have keen a perception and/or discernment plus the responsibility for managing God's resources in God's way.

*Problems and Questions:*
Where can I fit in?
Who needs me?
Physical challenges increase.
Not wanting to be irrelevant.
How do I keep up with new ideas and technology?

# Reflective Sharing

**Reflective Sharing (88+)**

Late Retirement: The ability to reflect on life's experiences and lay out issues and principles in ways that will be helpful to subsequent generations. The benefits of longevity will be clear and the contribution to the well-being of those, especially those under 45, will be significant. As health deteriorates, wisdom accelerates.

*Wisdom, meaning, and serious and thoughtful insights are shared with those you care for.*

***Problems and Questions:***
Keeping energy up
Fighting a shrinking world
Loss of friends and loved ones
Focusing outward instead of inward

Each of the three stages previously referenced has unique characteristics and bring unique value to constructing the Kingdom. There is a special call on your life and it plays itself out in different ways during each of those stages. Listen for it. Pray about it. Act on it.

# Questions & Application

What could you see yourself doing during the ACTIVE APPLICATION stage of retirement:

_____

_____

_____

_____

What could you see yourself doing during the INSIGHTFUL STEWARDSHIP stage of retirement:

_____

_____

_____

_____

What could you see yourself doing during the REFLECTIVE SHARING stage of retirement:

_____

_____

_____

_____

# 4

## The Future Funded Ministry Attitude

The Future Funded Ministry attitude is empowering and uniquely identifiable. This dynamic attitude will empower you and encourage other Christians:

- Future Funded Ministry puts the focus on God's plan and your response.

- It is devoted to the devoted—we are all ministers together.

- It encourages the planning needed to help yourself serve God as a minister—a life changer.

- It enables missionaries, ministers, and church

employees as well as Christian organization workers to plan and wisely manage money during their income-producing years for years of future non-employer or support funded ministry.

- It prompts and empowers you to act now—to accept the fact that retirement does indeed happen in the future and it must be funded. Pre-funding it now will help you enjoy the fruits of your labor later and fill your life with meaningful purpose.

**Retirement Redefined:**

Future Funded Ministry is a message and a call for all Christians to continue building the Kingdom by listening carefully, reflecting deeply, and funding future ministry completely.

We have heard many excuses:

- "How can I afford to start with all the things I need to spend money on now just to live?"

- "I am too old to start."

- "What money do I have to save and invest?"

- "I just don't have enough money."

Typically, your financial landscape is bigger than the one you think you see every day. The investments that you have made over time may be right under your nose, dormant or growing slowly. Remember the growth of the mustard seed? Those seeds are all around you.

## Questions & Application

Have you ever considered preparing for retirement as a funding a future ministry (if not, explain why):

_____

_____

_____

_____

Do you agree with the concept of a Future Funded Ministry (explain your answer below):

_____

_____

_____

_____

If more Christians embraced a Future Funded Ministry, do you think it would change anything:

_____

_____

_____

_____

# 5

# Financial Landscape

As a first step, it is absolutely paramount that you determine your financial landscape. Start by surveying your financial situation. Next, it is important to clearly understand the scope of opportunities available to you.

You can think about your financial landscape as being composed of the following: assets, opportunities, plans, and applications. Assets alone do not make up a financial landscape—we are all too close to our obvious assets to understand true potential. For now, take a moment to explore and reflect on whether or not you have any of the following important items in your financial landscape:

- Do you own a house or any other real property?

- Do you have a car, boat, or recreational vehicle that is rarely used?

- Do you have an inheritance or perhaps one awaiting you from a trust or will?

- Do you have life insurance with a cash value or an annuity?

- Do you or your spouse currently have an IRA?

- Do you have money in a current or converted employer's retirement plan: 401(k), 403(b), 457, etc.?

- Do you have a pension from a denomination or organization?

- Do you know the most opportune time to access your social security?

- Do you regularly have a tax refund? What can you do with this refund?

- Are you currently receiving any additional income such as alimony, side business, or social security while you are over 65 and still working?

- Do you have a job currently, or are you willing to work?

- Is your spending prioritized? Has it been reviewed and evaluated?

**What Are Your Spending Patterns?**

It is critical to understand your spending patterns. One reason for its importance is that there is often "hidden spending" that we overlook or we minimize its impact. Gift giving and dry cleaning are two of those hidden expenses. Often you discount their drain on income and do not recognize that the few hundred spent each month on these "necessities" are diminishing your ability to pay off debt or maximize your savings.

**Your Saving Opportunities**

It is important to realize that while you are in your earning years, when your ministry organization or employer offers a retirement package or plan, opt in immediately. However little you contribute, it will be strategically important for you and your family when it comes to "living" and enjoying your retirement of meaning and purpose. No matter how little you contribute, starting now is critical (see the following diagram use a retirement calculator such as apps.finra.org/calcs/1/ retirement).

## Debts, Liabilities, Skills, and Capabilities

Your financial landscape also includes your debts and liabilities plus your skills and capabilities. Your liabilities, what you owe, is important because it restricts your choices and limits your options. Your liabilities create a barrier to moving forward and putting your Future Funded Ministry into motion.

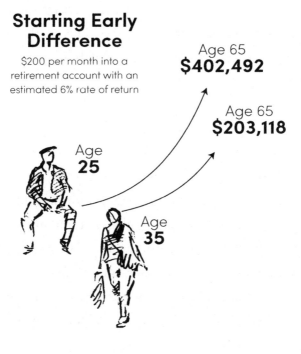

### Starting Early Difference

$200 per month into a retirement account with an estimated 6% rate of return

Age 65
**$402,492**

Age 65
**$203,118**

Age
**25**

Age
**35**

Liabilities create a psychological barricade keeping you from wrapping your head around your Future Funded Ministry and what it should look like. On the other hand, your talents, skills, and experiential learning capabilities form an important foundation for your financial landscape. This is your capacity to create value and thus to produce sustainable assets and usable resources. Simply stated, you will have more money.

We can't grow what we don't have like a victory garden during WWI. Fruits and vegetables were at a premium. Victory gardens provided nutrition and hope. Each of us has the comparable capacity, yet few of us fully use it. The good news is that God has prepared you for a future of service and will not withhold the ability to create it, to fulfill your Future Funded Ministry calling. He will both strengthen you as needed and uphold you as required to fulfill His purpose for your life.

**Easy Keys to a Sound Financial Landscape**

Here are some keys to help you set up your financial landscape—key elements to put your Future Funded Ministry into motion. On one hand, you might be thinking, "No kidding? Can I do this?" On the other hand, you should be asking yourself, "Am I really going to do this?" I trust your answer is "YES." Moving forward, here are the simple keys to savings:

- Live on what you make.

- Put a plan in place for getting out of debt.

- Understand how you and your spouse view money and make financial decisions. This is critical to both your planning and execution of the plan.

- Create a retirement plan and choose the investment vehicles that are most applicable to your risk profile, age, remaining time to retirement, money personality, and savings approach.

**Your Financial Landscape Defined**

In a nutshell, the assets you have, plus your on-going earnings, minus your current debt-level, along with the approach and plans that you and your spouse are creating together compose your financial landscape.

Each of us has a financial landscape. Now is the time

for you to acknowledge what it is, develop alternative action plans, and take charge of your future.

> ***Then you will know the truth,***
> ***and the truth will set you free.***
> John 8:32

# Financial Landscape = current assets + current earning - current debt + additional earning capacity

## Current Assets

Real-estate _____

Stocks & Bonds _____

Retirement _____

Savings _____

Other _____

*Total* _____

## Current Earnings

You _____

Spouse _____

2nd Source _____

*Total* _____

## Current Debt

Mortgage _____

Credit Cards _____

Car(s) _____

Medical _____

Other _____

*Total* _____

## Additional Earning Capacity

2nd Job _____

Business _____

Sales _____

Other _____

*Total* _____

## TOTAL

   Current Assets _____

+  Current Earning _____

-  Current Debt _____

+  Additional
Earning Capacity _____

= **Financial Landscape** _____

6

# Ages & Stages

## A Plan for Every Age and Life Stage

- Will you have enough? These are the common concerns expressed by people just like you every day:

- Will I have enough to pay for medical expenses and care?

- Will I have enough to pay my bills and live independently as long as I am physically able?

- Will I outlive _____ (you fill this in with the right answer for you)?

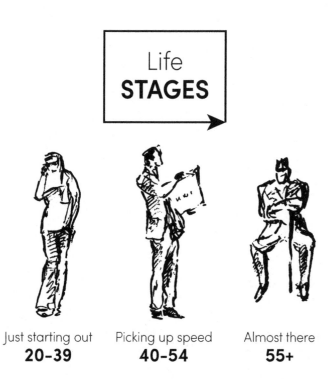

| Life **STAGES** → | | |
| --- | --- | --- |
| Just starting out **20-39** | Picking up speed **40-54** | Almost there **55+** |

Some people are rightfully nervous. Others really are on track to have a well-funded retirement that will allow them to live with financial peace and serve their Future Funded Ministry wherever they feel called. Often, they just don't know it.

But you won't have enough if you don't plan, and Que Sera Sera (whatever will be will be) is not a plan. The old adage says it best: "If you fail to plan, you plan to fail." And along with the right plan comes the right strategy to implement your plan. Being diligent and consistent over the years helps.

## The Key to Building a Winning Plan

The key to building a winning plan starts by looking at where you are today and making the right strategic decisions based on your stage of life. Starting early certainly helps your money to multiply and grow. The power of compounding explodes over a longer period of time.

Simply stated—you will retire, so recognizing where you are in your life as early as possible is the best approach to building a successful retirement. Planning for your Future Funded Ministry is essential. However, if you start later, you can still make smart choices increasing the likelihood that you will retire with enough—and if not enough, at least more than you would have if you did not start at all.

**Starting is important. Starting early is best.**

## Other Kinds of Preparation Are Important Too

It is important to note that preparing "financially" is not the only preparation for you to begin sooner rather than later. Physical, emotional, and spiritual preparations are equally important. We all tend to focus on the lack of money because it's the most obvious piece missing if you don't prepare. Even if you have "enough" money but have not recognized the value of these other factors, you will be prevented from carrying out God's assignment and your very personal mission.

When we reflect on our responsibility to steward all of God's resources, money and physical resources come to mind immediately. Our broad stewardship responsibility covers a lot more geography. We are all stewards of our physical being, passions, emotions, and of course our spirituality. We are responsible for the decisions we make and the roles we plan to stay connected to God. Thankfully, He makes His power and wisdom available to us when we are operating in His will and for His glory.

It is beyond the scope of this book to explore these other key elements of Future Funded Ministry. The book, *Finding Freedom*, certainly encompassed many of these vital factors. In the next book, we will explore what it means to be "faithful" during each season of life and then explore how we can know our calling. Look for it.

Let's start by recognizing what is true about your age and life stage. The following chapters include some financial tips based on different ages and stages of life. You either took these steps when you were younger or wish you had. Understanding what makes sense during earlier life stages will help you give leadership and/or wise counsel to those God has or will put in your path—those you may advise, mentor, or simply model a lifetime of faithful stewardship.

## Advantages for Pastors, Ministers, and Missionaries

All those who are properly licensed, commissioned, or ordained by an ecclesiastical body can take a minister's housing allowance, which gives the right to reduce their ministry-based income by an amount equal to the expenses associated with their housing costs. This benefit impacts your Future Funded Ministry plan in two ways:

1. During your active ministry years, you pay significantly less SECA tax. Make sure you save the difference and set it aside in your retirement plan for 4th Quarter ministry funding.

2. During your retirement years, you can take distributions equal to your housing allowance from your 403(b)(9) retirement plan without paying taxes. Functionally, this is an increase in compensation equal to your tax bracket—maybe as much as 25% at that point in time.

All voluntary contributions you make to your 403(b)(9) retirement plan reduces your SECA (The Self Employment Contribution Act) tax, as well as your state and federal income tax. The SECA tax is paid by those with ministerial status who have not opted out of Social Security. For those who have not opted out, the increased savings is in the 15.3% range, in addition to normal retirement savings. Again, this provides an immediate tax savings of about 15.3%. Make sure to reinvest those tax savings back into your 403(b)(9) retirement plan account. Compounding, remember?

For missionaries living overseas for over 50% of the year, contributions made to your retirement plan that are not made by your employer or ministry can go into an after-tax Roth account. This means that when following the ROTH regulations, you will never pay tax on that money. Because of the Overseas Income Credit, you typically cannot contribute to a Roth IRA, but you can contribute to a Roth 403(b).

By understanding the tax code and the regulations that pertain to both those with ministerial status and/ or overseas missionary status, your Future Funded Ministry during the 4th Quarter can be significantly enhanced and put into motion sooner.

This outline is only intended to alert you to the possibilities available. Please consult your tax professional for further details.

# Questions & Application

Why is it important to understand your current and future life stages?

_____

_____

_____

_____

If you are a pastor, minister, or missionary, what are some unique financial advantages available to you?

_____

_____

_____

_____

When is the best time to start preparing financially?

_____

_____

_____

_____

_____

_____

7

## Just Starting Out: Ages 20-39

Enroll in pre-tax 403(b), 457, or 401(k) defined contribution plans. These plans may offer contributions
into your account by your employer; they may also
have a "matching" component. In both situations,
there is "free" money, so don't miss out. Lastly, your
own contribution is often from pre-tax income, and
those deductions help you save immediately on income taxes so make sure to re-invest those tax savings
too—you won't miss them!

At a minimum, employer retirement plans help you
deduct money pre-tax from your paycheck and de-
posit it into a diversified investment portfolio. Those
monies can either be managed by you or a profession-

al services firm who can do it for you. The benefits of many employer-sponsored plans include a "free" money component—an employer match or even direct contribution without a match—plus additional tax advantages. For instance, "the match" can range from 25% to 100% of what you contribute, to a maximum of 6% of your salary. Even if the match is at the low end, it's an immediate 25% return on your investment. You're not going to get that kind of return anywhere else. Start now or increase what you are already contributing.

An additional strategy is to put your contributions into a Roth account. You will give up preset tax savings but never pay taxes on the distributions—the amounts you take out. For many, this is a great benefit. Participation in these types of savings plans is a key step towards funding your Future Funded Ministry. Remember that power of compounding? It is now working for you.

It's important to realize that the money you contribute to your 403(b) or 401(k) is excluded from taxable income—your specified amount is deducted from your pre-tax earnings and is a great way to save large chunks of money without feeling as much of the pain of savings. Once you take the tax break into account, a 6% contribution feels like 4.5%.

## Fund a Roth IRA

If you don't have a 403(b) or 401(k) plan available, fund an IRA. Many small employers, ministries, or faith-based organizations don't have the money or experience to offer a retirement plan at all, let alone one with either a basic or matching contribution. This means you have to start your own retirement plan. Like the 403(b) or 401(k), an IRA can accommodate either pre-tax contributions (you save taxes now) or Roth contributions (you save taxes later).

For most young workers and some older ones (for example ministers that take advantage of Minister's Housing Allowance to reduce their taxable income), a realistic and tax-free choice is to start a Roth IRA or a Roth 403(b). Contributions aren't tax-deductible, but you can withdraw the principle from them tax-free. As long as you wait until you're age 59 1/2 to take withdrawals, earnings are tax-free too. Funding a Roth IRA is a good idea, even if you are contributing to an employer's retirement plan.

As of 2017, you can invest up to $5,500 if you are under age 50 and $6,500 if you are 50 and older in a Roth IRA. You can contribute a significantly greater amount into a 403(b), 403(b)(9), and others. You do not need $5,500 or even a $1,000 to get started in an IRA. Make sure to check the current amount because this could fluctuate from year to year depending on the IRS.

An automatic investment program, such as a 401(k) or a 403(b), is one where you continue to invest into the account monthly and it can be started with much less. Typically, 401(k) and 403(b) plans do not have a minimum monthly savings requirement so there are few reasons not to participate. Even if you forgo one pizza a month and invest the savings, you are pointed in the right direction.

## Student Loans

Don't worry about quickly paying off your student loans unless the interest rate is really high. It is important to realize that $2,500 of a student loan's interest is tax deductible. Also, interest rates are often fixed and fairly low—between 3.4% and 6.8% for loans issued after 2006. Keeping them and paying them off slowly makes sense. Of course, like any debt, it is better to eventually pay them off than to have them. Make sure you pay off your higher interest loans first. This strategy will make a real impact on your financial landscape by helping you pay off debt faster and save for the future sooner.

## No Cashing Out!

Resist cashing out a retirement account. When you leave a job, you have several options. You can leave your account with your former employer, roll it into an IRA, roll it into your new employer's plan (if your employer permits such rollovers), or ask your former employer to cut you a check. You may be tempted to choose the last option, but in most cases, that's a bad idea.

Your employer will follow IRS regulations and with-hold 20% of the amount withdrawn to cover income taxes. And because you're under 59 1/2, you'll also have to pay a 10% early-withdrawal penalty. Plus, you're jettisoning any growth you've earned, which sends you back to square one when you start saving again. Workers who cash out their 401(k) or 403(b) plans reduce their retirement income by up to 67%, according to an analysis by the Employee Benefit Research Institute.

The following personal story of mine illustrates how misplaced priorities can impact future ministry. During my time in Graduate School in Berkeley, my wife Judy taught 3rd grade in the San Leandro, California school district. I was working on my MBA, and Judy was supporting both of us. During that time Judy accumulated some funds in the retirement plan for the school district. It amounted to a little over $2,000, which was about 1/3 of a year's salary at that time. Yes, it was a long time ago.

Upon graduation, we were going to move to Dearborn, Michigan, and I was going to work for the Ford Motor Company. We had little money and virtually no furniture. Judy had patiently waited during these early years of marriage for the furniture that I promised her was on the horizon. Yes, you guessed it. We took the money out of the retirement account, paid the taxes, and bought furniture.

Many years later, when reflecting on that decision, I calculated what the value of that money would be now if we had not taken it out and bought furniture.

Based on my assumption about the rate of return, it amounted to close to $50,000. The furniture is long gone, and so is the amount that we would have now to put into our Future Funded Ministry account. Expensive furniture, right?

## Money for a House

Siphon off cash for a down payment. As untouchable as retirement accounts should normally be, a loan from your retirement account can be a good idea. You can repay the loan over 30 years, under most plans when the loan is intended to help with the down payment for a principal residence, and the interest you pay goes back into your same retirement account. To justify this strategy, you need to have enough time before retirement to repay the loan and replenish the accounts. Also, be strategic about which investment account you tap. Take the money from the conservative portion of your investment portfolio. For example, the interest you are paying back to yourself can replace a bond fund or money market fund.

## Borrowing from Your Retirement Plan

You can often borrow against your 403(b) or 401(k)—an option not available with IRAs. You may borrow as much as half of the money in your account—up to $50,000. That borrowing can be for any reason. But it better be a good one. You must repay your 401(k) or 403(b) loan within five years. The amount not paid back as prescribed is then taxed by the IRS in the following year.

Your employer or retirement plan provider may allow you to take as long as 30 years to pay back the loan if you're borrowing to purchase a primary residence, as mentioned above. Loans are usually repaid through payroll deduction. So remember, if you are going to leave your current employment, make sure you are able to pay back the loan before you leave. Otherwise, there will be a large tax bill right ahead of you.

If you chose to withdraw money from the account rather than borrow it, you could incur taxes and a 10% penalty. Borrowing can be better. If you withdraw money from an IRA, Uncle Sam waives the 10% penalty on a distribution of up to $10,000 for a first-time home buyer, although you'll still owe taxes on the withdrawal. If your spouse is also a first-time home buyer, you can each withdraw up to $10,000 penalty-free, but not tax free.

Already own your home? Consider refinancing your mortgage for a lower interest rate. The rule of thumb is that refinancing is the viable option when the interest rate you are currently paying can be reduced by 1% or more. It is important to put the savings generated by a lower house payment into your retirement account. If you do, this is a good strategy. If you don't, it's not.

**$100,000 at 6% = $500 monthly and $100,000 at 4% = $333 monthly. Save the $167 difference over 30 years, and it equals $167,000 (assuming 6% return).**

All of the previous suggestions are ways to improve your stewardship and leverage the resources God has entrusted to you. Check out the examples Jesus gave, recorded in Matthew 25, for additional insights into your stewardship responsibility and its accompanying results.

# Questions & Application

Since retirement is a long way away, do you think it is important to start saving now (why or why not):

_____

_____

_____

_____

What are some good first steps to take during this life stage:

_____

_____

_____

_____

Once you start saving for the future, what should you resist doing:

_____

_____

_____

_____

**8**

# Picking Up Speed: Ages 40-54

It's not too late to get started with your savings and investing plan, but here is the reality—you better get started. "Time it is a wasting." Here are the insights you need for success when starting during this life stage—three variables that determine how successful you will be at "growing money" (synonymous with investing):

1. Dollar amount invested (how much you save or invest)

2. Percentage rate of return (the rate at which the money grows)

3. The length of time for the money to grow (the

number of years before you plan to access the money)

I've shared these variables during hundreds of retirement planning workshops. Typically, I'll ask the listeners to rank those variables in order of importance to future money success.

Here are the normal responses in rank order:

1. I don't have any idea

2. The dollar amount invested

3. Rate of return on the money invested

4. Length of time the money has to grow

Interestingly, the correct answer is #4 (length of time) followed by #2 and then #3. Time is the most important variable. Most assume it is the dollar amount. That helps explain why so many give up on saving because they think their dollar amount is too low—why even bother? Because "time" is the most important, starting early is crucial. The more time between now and when the money needs to be available, the easier it is to save the total amount needed. It is critical to understand this priority and why starting now is better than starting later.

For example, here's the penalty for procrastinating on your retirement savings: If you had started saving for retirement in your twenties, you would have had to carve out 13% of your salary every year to replace your income in retirement, according to an analysis by T. Rowe Price. Now, at 40, you'll need to sock away 26-29% of your salary to catch up. And, if you put it off until age 55, you'll need to save 43%, which won't leave you much for groceries or gas.

Don't be discouraged—just get started. Or, if you've already started, keep contributing. If you can, try adding a little every year to the total amount being saved.

Because so many people wait too long, there are powerful government incentives that work in your favor once you're over 50. At 50 and above, you are permitted to contribute significantly more to your 403(b) or 401(k) plan than your younger colleagues. The current "catch-up" percent of your age (50) is $5,500 a year. Make sure to check the current amount because it does change occasionally.

There are many family and/or business situations

where more money is available to set aside during this life stage, particularly towards the end of it. These include a work bonus, a spouse that goes back to work, the death of a family member who has left money for you, and reduced expenses after a child leaves home.

## The Truth About Compounding

These three variables (amount, rate of return, and length of time) are the components of compounding. Einstein is purported to have said that compounding is the most powerful force in money and nature. Here is his actual quote, "Compound interest is the eighth wonder of the world. He who understands it, earns it ... he who doesn't ... pays it."

Question: What would you rather have—$200,000 or the value of a penny doubled for 30 days? Without more thought, most answer $200,000. Then, they start to figure it out: 1 penny, 2 pennies, 4 pennies, 8 pennies, 16 pennies, 32 pennies, 64 pennies, $1.28. By the 9th day, you have yielded a measly $2.56. Seems like a paltry return when the amount compounding stops after the 30th day.

Here is the shocker—your decision to take the

$200,000 will cost you over $5,000,000. The value of 1 penny doubled is $5,368,709 on day 30. I've always found this amazing! Go ahead, get out your calculator and figure it out yourself.

Now, you can amaze your family and friends with your depth of financial knowledge and acuity, or skill. Or, just sit back and be amazed.

## Prepare for Contingencies

If you have not done so already, fuel an emergency fund with enough money to cover at least six month's worth of basic expenses. This cushion helps keep you solvent after a layoff and prevents you from borrowing your way out of a crisis. The key is to have access, not necessarily cash on hand, for up to 6 month's worth of expenses. Putting an extra amount into your retirement fund and designating it for emergencies is one approach. You access the monies by borrowing.

## Contribute as Much as You Can

Make it a priority to contribute at least 10% of your gross income into retirement savings. In addition, ministers and missionaries can take advantage of their special tax incentives. Overseas missionaries enjoy tax-free income because of the foreign earned income exclusion. With no taxes to be paid up to the limit, a contribution to a Roth 403(b) is an astute savings strategy. Voluntary retirement contributions by licensed, ordained, or commissioned ministers are also Pre-SECA.

This yields an immediate tax savings of 15.3% (applicable to ministers who have not opted out of social security). Here is the key—make sure you contribute the amount of the tax savings to your retirement account. The next important step is to use your housing allowance distribution option after retirement. Unfortunately, many clergies either do not know or understand the value of this option and transfer money out of a 403(b)(9) to an IRA, losing the benefit entirely.

## Plan for Children's College Education

We all know that there is a big difference in the cost of education depending on where you send your children to college. Much of the decision on where to go, and therefore the expense, is dependent upon a realistic matching of your child/children to interests, capacity, and innate capability.

What will be their life or career track: Liberal arts? Business? Vocational school? Also, there is the very real possibility your child is not wired to either enjoy or benefit from a 4-year college degree. Matching applicable education with the appropriate expense only makes sense. Our culture and sometimes our pride get in the way of making good decisions.

There are new apprenticeship programs popping up, particularly in high-tech manufacturing areas. In another career direction, great education leading to a teaching degree can be found across the spectrum of colleges with the associated range of tuition. My undergraduate degree from the Ohio State University in History and an MBA from Berkeley have served me well. They matched both my capability and capacity to pay. Fortunately, Judy's teaching job paid for graduate school much to my parent's relief. Regardless of the cost, the same time-and-money crunch applies to college savings that applies to retirement savings.

Also, the amount of student loan debt in our country is appalling. We need to be better stewards of our resources in this arena. So often we let a false pride get in our way when we say we want "only the best for our kids." Perhaps we need to examine what is best from a stewardship of time, money, and outcome.

Compare the difference between starting a college fund when your child is a toddler versus waiting until he or she is 13.

Starting earlier, you would have to save $345 a month to cover 75% of the cost of a public college education, according to Savingforcollege.com. Because you waited—you delayed saving for five years — you'll have to save $646 a month. That's almost twice as much!

Rather than regret the past, recalibrate the present. If you are on track for retirement but short of the needed education savings amount, you can always redirect 1% or 2% of your gross income from one pot, retirement, to the other for a few years. Recognize that this can result in you working a year or two longer before retirement or boost the savings for retirement after you're done paying the college bills.

Or consider borrowing—judiciously of course. Parent PLUS loans, sponsored by the federal government, carry a fixed 7.9% rate. PLUS loans let you borrow up to the cost of tuition minus any financial aid. However, remember that borrowing on behalf of your student can jeopardize your own financial security in retirement. If the gap is a chasm, not a crevice, find a less expensive school.

Another way to get cash for college is to borrow against the equity in your home. With a home-equity loan, you pay a fixed rate (recent average: 6.4%). If you decide to go that route, borrow the entire amount upfront if the interest rate is low and fixed. With a line of credit, you pay a variable rate (recent average: 5.1%) and then borrow as needed. With both, you can generally deduct the interest on amounts borrowed up to $100,000, no matter how you use the money.

Other smart alternatives include making a fixed amount of money available to your child (children) for college. For example, an amount that will cover four years at a local college or only one year at an out of state school. For most, a college degree is what is important not the school's name written on the diploma.

Paul followed his parent's urging to apply to a private college and was accepted. Total yearly expense was $65,000 with half of that in student loans. Mom and Dad were so proud. Paul was miserable. He stuck it out for two years and then enlisted in the Army. He carried with him $65,000 worth of debt and received little long-term value. Perhaps another strategy would have yielded better results. Make sure you are using the "truth" about your children and your finances when deciding on any next steps, especially when it comes to education.

Scott decided to go to a junior college for his first two years. His parents thought a private school education was important but supported his decision. After two years at the junior college, a 4.0 GPA and significant extra-curricular activities, Scott applied for and was accepted to the same school that Paul was just leaving. After two more years, he did have college debt of $65,000, but he had an outstanding college degree that set him up for graduate school in a profession that was the right fit for him.

Talk honestly with your kids. Let them know what you are prepared to contribute for college expenses before they make up a college wish list. Be clear that if the net price after financial aid doesn't end up at your number, it has to go off the list. Without this conversation, you'll be hard-pressed to say "no" when the acceptance letter from an expensive University comes. Make sure only clear, straightforward truth is in play when it comes to making these hard choices about "higher" education for your children. It is hard, but necessary, to isolate the issues when there are multiple personalities and emotions in the decision-making room.

Often grandparents are financially able and want to contribute to the costs of college. Speak frankly with them a year or so before the college selection process starts. Transparency and clear communication will yield the best for you, the grandparents, and the grandchild.

Understanding the money personalities of all the participants in the, "where to go to college" conversation will go a long way towards family unity and making great, not just good, decisions. The Saver-Security Seeker will most likely favor the community college while the Spender-Risk Taker will opt for Stanford, and the Flyer won't even care about what it costs.

It is usually not the amount of money you have, or don't have, that causes the arguments about money, but how the money is going to be used, spent, invested, or wasted. To begin unpackaging these issues, you can find the Money Personality assessment at bruce-bruinsma.com/moving-forward-resources. Not only does knowing your Money Personality save marriages, but it also saves family relationships. In a later section, we do a deep dive into the Money Personalities.

## Addressing the Wedding Conundrum

A father came to see me and wanted a $50,000 loan against his retirement plan to help fund his only daughter's wedding. Note: I did not say, his daughter's only wedding. In addition, he borrowed an equal amount against his home. So, they had a $100,000 wedding.

While I cautioned him against spending that much, especially after he explained the events surrounding the short-lived relationship between the two young people being married, he was insistent and took out both loans. The wedding ceremony was spectacular. And yes, you guessed it, about 7 months later he came to my office again, severely depressed. The young couple had recently filed for divorce. And yes, he still owed the $100,000.

How much better to agree upon a reasonable limit to spend on the wedding and make that amount clear to your son or daughter. That amount is certainly dependent upon your financial capacity and the marriage situation, but clearly setting financial boundaries is a good idea.

With the high divorce rate, even among those of faith, the finances surrounding weddings are complicated. Who pays what, and when do they pay often leads to more stress than the circumstance can sustain. Clear understandings, clear boundaries, and clear dollar amounts will reduce inter-family stress. They might even save marriages.

## Invest What's Left

If you're among those who have college and wedding commitments covered (or don't have those costs to contend with), you are already saving the max in your retirement accounts each year, you may be one of the few looking for ways to invest excess income. Here are a few great options:

Add tax-free municipal bonds to your fixed-income allocation. Despite recent reports, most state and local governments have shown resilience in the face of budget cuts. With rising interest rates, Christian Credit Unions also have attractive investments and lower risk savings options.

One thought is that if your student is heading off to college, you can accomplish multiple goals (and take advantage of a strong rental market) by buying a condo near campus and letting your young adult and a few roommates live in it. The underlying principle is to leverage each situation as it comes, along with the notion, as the saying goes, to explore whether there is lemonade amongst the lemons. Later, rent that property to other students or alumni that will generate income for and into your retirement.

# Questions & Application

If you have not started saving for retirement, is it too late:

_____

_____

_____

_____

How can children affect your financial planning and preparation:

_____

_____

_____

_____

What are some options for investing extra income once you have maxed out your retirement plan:

_____

_____

_____

_____

9

# Almost There: Age 55+

At this time, retirement isn't a far-off goal you'll worry about someday when you're ready for your second hip replacement. Unless you plan to work until you drop, retirement is staring you in the face. In our recent survey, over 65% of respondents in this age bracket were concerned about not having enough monthly income for their retirement years. Think of how a lack of funds affects your stewardship. Your Future Funded Ministry is certainly at risk.

Obviously, this is the time to get serious and become engaged about saving. You are aware, maybe even a little scared, if you haven't saved enough. And that's true for most people! According to The Balance, the average amount saved for those who are 50 to 55 is

$124, 831 ("Average Retirement Savings," 2018). You don't need a calculator to realize that $124,000 is not enough.

A recently released study from the Employee Benefit Research Institute suggests that nearly half (47%) of "early boomers"—those between the ages of 56 and 62—will run out of money during retirement ("Retirement Income Preparation," 2010). For many, these are still prime earning years, and some of your significant expenses—such as a down payment on a home and college tuition—are behind you.

To make sure you are on track, don't hesitate to seek help from a financial planner or use the many calculators available online. There are an increasing number of advisory services often termed "Robo Advisors" that can bring financial clarity to your situation. Here is one more instance where "The truth will set you free" is relevant. Unfortunately, there is a lot of advice available, but not all of it is helpful. Solomon suggested wisdom and prudence in all things. His advice is applicable in this circumstance too.

As mentioned in the last section, once you are 50 or older, you can contribute thousands more to your 401(k) or 403(b) plan than your younger colleagues.

You can contribute an additional amount of money over the annual limit. Any employer contribution on top of that is gravy. Go to IRS.gov for the current limit.

*And don't stop there.*

In 2012, the IRS started allowing catch-up contributions to Roth IRAs. Unlike a traditional IRA, you don't have to take annual minimum withdrawals from a Roth once you turn 70 1/2.

However, there are income limits on Roth IRA contributions. You are eligible for this benefit if your modified adjusted gross income is less than $125,000 ($183,000 if you're married and file jointly). Again, there are IRA limitations on contribution amounts while there are much higher limitations with 401(k) and 403(b) plans. By the way, churches have a special type of plan, a 403(b)(9) church plan. This is the best option for churches and those with ministerial status.

## Dare to Downsize

You may have hoped to move to smaller living accommodations as soon as the kids were grown. Some homeowners, who have watched the value of their homes decline in recent years, are reluctant to sell until the real estate market rebounds. Even if your home hasn't returned to its former value, moving to a smaller, less expensive home can save you thousands of dollars a year in taxes, utility costs, and insurance.

These savings can be funneled into retirement savings. You may need some help with this approach but do the financial analysis and make a wise decision. An accountant can help you with the math.

Figuring out the location and the size of your future housing are critical decisions. For example, over a 13-year period, Judy and I downsized from a house to a condo, and then to an apartment. Each move brought with it both advantages and issues. Our apartment was 1200 square feet. Judy loves to economize and is great at throwing things out, so it worked well for her. Not so much for me. I'm neither as adept at discarding things nor as petite as Judy.

When we decided to move to Colorado Springs we took a different tack. We bought a lot and built our first house. It is more than three times bigger than our apartment, is situated in a forest, and we both love it. See, there are many twists and turns to everyone's "living" stories. No, it was not cheaper for us but is the way we have chosen to position the second stage of our "retirement" years.

## Consolidate Your Orphaned 403(b) or 401(k) Plans

You've probably changed jobs several times and you may still have money in former employers' retirement plans. Leaving money in a former employer's plan is not as bad as cashing it out. But as you approach retirement, it is a good idea to consolidate your savings into one IRA. There is another step you can take prior to retirement, and that is to consolidate your retirement accounts with one vendor.

Then, upon retirement, it will be easier to move to an IRA. Or, you may leave the account with that final vendor. You will get a better handle on how much money you have and where it's invested by consolidating your accounts. You will also have more investment choices and pay lower administrative expenses. Once you start taking withdrawals, it will be easier to take them from your IRA than from a former employer's plan. For example, some financial services make an "Anchor" IRA available. This is an excellent place to aggregate all of your retirement plan monies.

Don't forget, if you have ministerial status, you need to leave the money in your 403(b)(9) account to take advantage of the Housing Allowance Distribution.

## Consider Long-Term Care Insurance

A well-funded retirement savings plan could be decimated in a matter of months if you end up in a nursing home or require round-the-clock home health care. Medicare doesn't cover the cost of long-term care and Medicaid isn't available until you've spent down most of your savings. Long-term care insurance could prevent this from happening, but make sure it fits your budget before making such a purchase. The costs are often high. You will have to pay premiums for many years and the cost of those premiums could increase significantly as insurers are confronted with the cost of providing long-term care to millions of aging baby-boomers. If you do not take out long-term-care insurance, set aside or allocate 3-5 years of the monthly cost of assisted care living expenses in your area of the country.

## Weigh Your Social Security Options

You are eligible to file for social security benefits when you turn 62, but if you do, your monthly check will be reduced significantly for the rest of your life. You may have little choice if you are out of work or in poor health and need the money to pay expenses. But if you have the wherewithal to work a few more years or have other sources of income, delaying checks until age 66, or your full benefit age, will increase your monthly amount by 33% or more.

That's not the only way working longer can boost your payouts. Your social security benefits are based on your highest 35 years of earnings. If you are a highly paid employee, working longer will displace some of your lower-earning years. You can see the Social Security Administration online tool that allows you to review your earnings record and get an estimate of your benefits. You should review this record annually because unreported or under-reported earnings reduce your monthly payments. To get your online statement, go to ssa.gov/mystatement.

If you work and get paid until age 70 and you start

taking your full social security benefit at age 66, you can save four years of social security payment into your pretax or Roth retirement account. What a difference this makes! I've noticed that for many, these are the most important savings years, making the difference between "not enough" and "enough."

Re-assess what you will spend in retirement. Most people underestimate how much they will spend when they retire. However, some financial planners and retirement calculators advise much more than you will need. While you may save on dry cleaning and commuting costs, you will still need to pay for groceries, utilities, and gas. If you refinanced to take cash out of your home, you may still have mortgage payments. And even after you're eligible for Medicare, you will spend some money on health care costs. Fidelity Investments estimates that the average 65-year-old couple will spend $260,000 on health care in retirement ("Health Care Costs," 2016). Still convinced you can live on less?

Here is a good idea—try living on your projected retirement income for 6 months while you are still working. This exercise will force you to evaluate your spending and cut back if needed. That means you'll be able to save more. And at this point in your life, saving is one of the few things you can control.

## Earn Supplemental Income

You can also supplement your earnings by working and/or consulting part time in your area of expertise. In retirement, you can get paid for doing your favorite hobby. You could work part-time in an area of expertise. All you have to do is be creative and energetic. Think of how you can use your knowledge and skills to earn additional income. At 97 years of age, Billy Graham received royalties on the book he wrote many years back.

# Questions & Application

How do (or could) you feel about your financial approach to retirement during this life stage:

_____

_____

_____

_____

What contribution advantage do you have once you have passed age 50:

_____

_____

_____

_____

Is it too late to consider supplemental income after 50:

_____

_____

_____

_____

# 10

## Discover Your Money Personality

The 5 Money Personalities were developed to give you insights into how to think about and deal with money plus understand why it is that you are the way you are when it comes to money. This section on understanding your money personality will help you build a foundation and remove barriers to what it takes for you to build your Future Funded Ministry. True money relationship success lays the groundwork for your Future Funded Ministry plan.

The 5 Money Personalities were designed by the Money Couple™, Scott and Bethany Palmer, in partnership with Dr. Kirk Cameron, Ph.D. in statistics—Stanford University. Cameron is the founder and president of

MacStat Consulting, Ltd. This statistical consulting firm specializes in scientific data analysis, statistical design, and statistical applications.

**Take your Money Personality Assessment now at bruoebruinsma.com/moving-forward-resources**

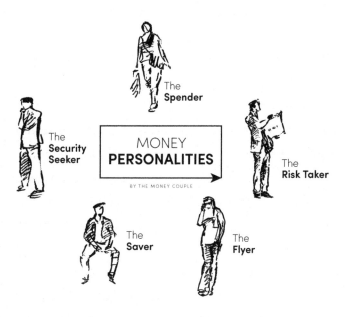

It is worth the pause in your reading to learn what is true about your money personality.

Each of us has two distinct money personalities—a primary or dominant money personality and a secondary one that hits close to home but is not as powerful as the primary one. To help you better understand this important concept, the following explanation is divided into three helpful parts.

1. **Know and Compare**

   Determine your distinct primary and secondary money personalities and then discover your partner's or spouse's primary and secondary money personalities, as well. Use this information to compare and chart your family dynamic.

2. **Identify**

   It is important to identify and understand the pros and cons of your opposite dynamics.

3. **Discover and Learn**

   In this part, you will reconcile your individual money personality with that of your partner. Next, you will reconcile the opposing forces that exist within your relationship. Once everyone is on the same page, you can build a healthy family dynamic.

Knowing your unique Money Personality Profile and understanding your spouse's Money Personality Profile is an important first step into learning how to approach your Future Funded Ministry Plan and investment portfolio. If you haven't already taken the Money Personality Assessment, do it now.

## PART 1:
## Know and Compare Your Money Personalities

There are five distinct money personalities. If you have read this far, by now you should have taken your assessment and identified your individual Money Personalities (have your spouse do it as well). The names of the 5 Money Personality types reflect their character. Let's take a moment and learn about some of the traits of each.

## Spender

Enough is never enough. Spenders can't help them-selves. They see or make up any excuse to open their wallet and get that new, next best thing. In fact, it doesn't have to be the latest, the greatest, it just has to be there in front of them and they are ready to jump for it.

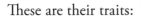

The **Spender**

These are their traits:

- Live in the moment

- Love to buy things for other people

- Get a thrill from the purchase

- Impractical and impulsive

- Non-communicative—come across as sneaky

- Filled with regret

- Budget breaker

**Risk Taker**

Your typical "Type A" personality. Fearless and often undaunted, the Risk Taker will choose the uncommon path because they cannot deny the need they are trying to fill.

The Risk Taker

The common traits of Risk Takers are:

- Big picture people

- Love finding the next adventure

- Get excited by the possibility

- Listen to their gut

- Unafraid to make decisions

- Sees endless possibilities

- Easily resented by others

- Inpatient and often insensitive

**Flyer**

Absolutely unemotional when it comes to money,
Flyers are often antsy to get on with the next thing
in their life. They are the defini-
tion of do what feels right but
not at the cost of relationships.
Perceived as irresponsible,
Flyers are actually more unor-
ganized and less intentional in
their lack of responsibility than
people who ignore responsibility altogether.

The
**Flyer**

Here are their common traits:

- Basically content with their lives
- Big on relationships—they thrive on connec-
  tions
- Happy to let someone else take care of their
  finances
- Not motivated by money
- Reactionary
- Lacking in the skills needed to solve money
  problems
- Disorganized and irresponsible when it comes
  to money

## Saver

"Good deal" lover and debt destroyer. Savers look for any chance to deny spending. They would rather squeeze everything they can from the things they have then get something new.

The **Saver**

Savers usually have some or all of these common traits:

- Get a genuine rush from saving money

- Are organized, responsible, and trustworthy when it comes to finances

- Rarely spend impulsively

- Avoid credit card debt

- Commonly referred to as "joy stealer"

- Overly focused on financial goals

- Cheap

**Security Seeker**

"The safer the better" is the mantra here. If it is consistent, predictable and safe, a Security Seeker will most likely save regularly. They will spend with joy when an opportunity becomes "a no brainer," otherwise it is always better to be safe than sorry. Security Seekers share these traits:

The **Security Seeker**

- An investigator

- Trustworthy

- Willing to sacrifice

- Prepared for anything

- Often overly negative

- Get stuck in a research rut

- Stifle creativity

As mentioned earlier, if you have taken the Money Personality Assessment. you already know which personality is your primary and which is your secondary. Again, it is important for your spouse to take the assessment. Your money personality is your lens to view life and understand it. This is the first step in strategizing your Future Funded Ministry plan. Now it is important to look at which Money Personality types are diametrically opposed.

## PART 2:
## Identify the Opposite Dynamic and Understand Strengths and Weaknesses

Money personalities frame your life. If you notice the different shared traits for each money personality, most are not only descriptive of the way you approach money but are descriptive of the way you are motivated from within and impact many decisions and responses.

Your primary money personality, the one that really drives your thinking about money, is always at the forefront. It is the easy one, the instinctive one, the one that drives your first impulse to act. Interestingly, it is the secondary money personality that is surprisingly powerful. It lets you feel the impact of your money choices.

Sometimes both parties to the relationship have similar primary and secondary money personalities. You might be both a Saver and a Security Seeker (grouped together because both look at money as an end and both are intentional about their acts). You might both be a Spender/Risk Taker, Flyer/Spender, or Flyer/Risk Taker grouped together because money is a means to an end. They are impulsive, experiencing little anxiety about consequences).

This mutual alignment smooths the financial decision making and eases the money discussions. If you and your spouse have diametrically opposed or simply opposite money personalities, some big money challenges may arise. Let's briefly examine what that means.

The opposite dynamic occurs when your primary money personality is in one aligned group of money personality characteristics and your secondary money personality is in the other group. In this case, your secondary money personality works as a kind of stop-gap that keeps your primary money personality from being too controlling. When the two are in opposition, there are some challenges as well as possible advantages, depending on which traits define your distinct money personality.

Most of us intuitively understand how two opposing forces can be a challenge. The following example shows us where the opposite dynamic becomes an advantage or at least allows an individual to live without regret and in balance.

Claire's primary money personality is a Saver, and her Secondary Money personality is a Flyer. Your first thought is that there is probably some major conflict going on inside of Claire. It is good that Claire's primary money personality is not a spender or there could be real trouble ahead—unpaid bills, deep debt, and maybe a foreclosure or two.

Claire, though, has the opposite dynamic which works in her favor. Being a Saver helps keep her from spending money she doesn't have. At the same time, her Flyer personality keeps her from falling into a spiral of remorse when she does spend more than normal. So, when Claire got a new job, that shopping spree she took made the Saver in her worry, yet by the afternoon the Flyer helped her move on, understanding that money isn't the only value in life.

If you have the opposite dynamic between your primary and secondary money personalities, it will take some time and reflection to understand how that discordance can become an advantage in your life. But once you see the give and take, how the tension plays itself out, you can understand that there is balance to be gained. That balance will help you approach money more effectively.

Identifying your aligned money personality or understanding how to effectively manage your opposite dynamic will help shape your approach to your Future Funded Ministry Plan. Now, let's take a deeper look at how the 5 Money Personalities work together to help you and your spouse get on the same page.

## PART 3:

## Discover How Money Personalities Work Together to Build the Family Dynamic

This information is critical to putting your Future Funded Ministry into motion because money fights with your spouse destroy the best of plans. Money fights don't lead to an effective Future Funded Ministry plan.

Fighting about money is the single most common and damaging problem experienced by most married couples and partnerships. Understanding your money relationship helps make sense of the underlying predicaments caused by having both similar and different primary and secondary money personalities vying for attention in a relationship.

Think about it—there are a lot of factors. There are two money personalities for each person; each person has a primary and secondary personality. From there, they can have very well aligned or opposed money personalities at work as individuals. And wait, there are two people involved so that complicates everything twice as much. The math becomes unwieldy. Let's try and make sense of this.

The first thing to do is to use this helpful chart to list your money personalities. Use this one or draw your own and then place your names and appropriate money personalities in the spaces below.

## Your Money Personalities

| | My Name | Spouse |
|---|---|---|
| Primary | | |
| Secondary | | |

Now that you've done it, here is a little secret—this chart is your money relationship and is everything you need to know to start working on your co-approach to speaking the same love and money language.

The first time you write it all down, it should be a revelation—an "oh that's why we bought the house," or "that's why we can't agree on what car we should get next." This chart helps you understand why you are arguing or having little disagreements, or why you have it pretty easy when it comes to financial decision making, or most likely somewhere in between.

Here are some things to remember to help whip your money relationship into better shape:

**Learn the Language**
Bridge the language barrier between you and your spouse by understanding what your primary and secondary money personalities mean and how they truly define the two of you.

**Walk a Mile**
If you are struggling to understand your spouse's or friend's money personalities, why not take a day and live out your life as if you were in their shoes? Don't go crazy but consider how they would make decisions and see it from their vantage point.

**Seeing What's Real**
The key to healthy relationships is accepting that you and your partner have different forces at work. We are all uniquely and wonderfully made. Keeping that in mind and accepting it will lead to better communication. Better communication will lead to more open and transparent discussions resulting in a new togetherness. Perhaps it will lead to the relationship you've

always dreamed about but never experienced.

With thanks to Scott and Bethany Palmer, we've only scratched the surface surrounding money personality issues. For a deeper understanding, we recommend going to TheMoneyCouple.com.

Acknowledging the importance of Money Personality is vital to understanding how you can plan your Future Funded Ministry and start thinking about an appropriate and comfortable investment portfolio.

# Questions & Application

What are some advantages of your Money
Personalities:

_____

_____

_____

_____

What are some disadvantages of your Money
Personalities:

_____

_____

_____

_____

How can understanding your Money Personalities
and those of others affect your relationship with your
spouse, kids, and others:

_____

_____

_____

_____

# 11

## Understanding Investment Terms and Risk

Before you can build a retirement plan or portfolio you must be able to talk the talk and walk the walk.

In this section, let's move from issues about money relationships to actual money issues. Let's tackle the basics together to understand how you are going to build that Future Funded Ministry plan—a successful plan, a customized Future Funded Ministry plan designed specifically for you.

To get there you need to 1) understand investment terminology, and 2) understand of your unique tolerance for risk.

## PART 1:

## Investment Terminology—the Rosetta Stone of Investing

In order to be a proficient investor, it's important to learn basic investment terminology. Let's call it the Rosetta Stone of Investing. Here is a good start:

### Portfolio

A portfolio is the collection or group of investments all owned by the same individual or organization. Your Future Funded Ministry needs a portfolio that matches your needs and reality. You will be able to define your customized portfolio, a selection of investments that is right for you, with some guidance and a deeper understanding of your money personalities, your money relationship, and your personalized risk indicator.

Every individual has a unique Future Funded Ministry and therefore needs an appropriate and sustainable portfolio to help fund it. "Sustainable" means a group of investments that you will stick with and not bail out of at the first sign of "down" or volatility.

**Stock**

Stock represents ownership in a company. Stocks are shares of a company and rise/fall within markets. Note that individual stocks are not investment options in 403(b) plans.

**Bond**

A bond is a loan to a company or government. Bonds are typically stable and turn pretty consistent interest rates. Individual bonds are not investment options in 403(b) plans.

**Mutual Fund/ETF**

Mutual Funds/ETFs are a pool of money from many investors that a professional money manager uses to buy the stocks and/or bonds of many different organizations. Your portfolio in your Future Funded Ministry plan will most likely be built on stocks, bonds, and savings.

**Volatility**

Volatility is both the up and down price movement of

your portfolio, which will most likely contain stocks, bonds, and mutual funds. The amount of the up and down, the volatility, is what causes retirement plan participants to make bad decisions.

## Risk

Risk is your tolerance for the degree of gain or loss, the "up and down" of an investment over time. Understanding your risk tolerance is essential to how you build and maintain your portfolio and make investment choices. Risk is also the key factor in determining your willingness to "stay with the investment" during the ups and downs of the market.

## Asset Allocation

Asset allocation is when you decide how much money to put into different asset classes or types of investments, at any given time. Investments can be conservative, moderate conservative, moderate, moderate aggressive, or aggressive. Much of your investment decisions will be about risk. Asset allocation is the foundation of investment management and the accompanying risk that comes with all investing. If you are not investing, you are simply saving, which brings a very low rate of return.

## Diversification

Diversification is the process of spreading your money among different kinds of investments. All investments have specific characteristics including what is being invested in, the volatility of the investment, and the strategy for picking each investment. Diversification is a key way to manage risk. You know the old saying, "Don't put all your eggs in one basket." Using different baskets reduces the risk that the eggs will be broken when your motor scooter tips over.

## Dollar Cost Averaging

Dollar cost averaging is investing the same dollar amount every month, regardless of market conditions and fluctuating prices. This is a systematic way to manage money because it forces you to buy low and sell high. Always a good idea.

## Compound Interest

Compound interest is best described as interest on interest. That is, interest calculated on the initial principal or amount invested and on the accumulated interest of previous periods. This is a powerful tool to increase and leverage your money. Compound interest is a powerful example of leverage. When you use something small to move something large, that's leverage. Another way of saying this is, "start with something small and watch it grow into something significantly larger." For example, a small paycheck deducted contribution to a retirement plan can grow into an amount large enough to fund your future ministry and lifestyle.

## PART 2:

## Understanding Risk

As learned in the previous section, "risk" is simply defined as the proportionate degree of gain or loss of any specific investment or portfolio. Risk is generally separated into three categories: (1) Conservative—least amount of risk, (2) Moderate—somewhat conservative and somewhat riskier, and (3) Aggressive—the riskiest strategies with riskier investments.

Generally speaking, more aggressive (higher risk) investments may deliver higher average returns over time. However, this is offset by a higher potential for loss of principal compared to safer, more conservative investments. That, of course, means the opposite is true as well—the less risky investment, the lower the risk of loss of principal and of course the lower potential for reward (lower return).

Everybody has a tolerance for risk equal to the three categories of risk: conservative, moderate, or aggressive. Our tolerance for risk impacts how we will react when an investment moves from up to down during its volatility cycle.

How do you know your risk tolerance? How much risk can you stand before you panic and make bad money decisions? You can determine your risk indicator, a number that signifies where you fall on a risk tolerance scale. You do this by answering a few key questions. Like your money personalities, knowing your risk indicator is important.

Your risk indicator will help you understand how to approach investment choices. When you determine your risk indicator and combine it with the way you see money (your money personalities), and then add your broader money relationships, those of your spouse or significant other, you will be able to determine the right approach to your Future Funded Ministry portfolio.

Let's take a few minutes to determine your risk level. How much volatility, up and down in the value of an investment, can you stand? A friend of mine often says how much "up" can you stand before you get "giddy" and how much "down" before you get an upset stomach. Let's start by determining your risk tolerance, which you can do online at brucebruinsma. com/moving-forward-resources.

If your investments mirror your tolerance for risk, it is more likely that you will persevere and create that sustainable portfolio previously described.

Now that you have discovered your money personalities, understand your money relationship, learned investment terms, and understand your risk indicator, you are ready to understand what it takes to build a financial investment plan. This is the heart of your Future Funded Ministry Plan and putting it into motion.

## Questions & Application

What are a few terms that you have heard before but never understood until reading this book:

_____

_____

_____

_____

Is it important for someone to understand these basic terms (why or why not):

_____

_____

_____

_____

What is your risk tolerance, and why is it important to know what it is:

_____

_____

_____

_____

# 12

## Asset Allocation and Building Your Future Funded Ministry Portfolio

There are different approaches to creating the best asset allocation model for yourself. Remember, an asset allocation model determines how much of your retirement money will be invested and where it will be invested—how your money will be divided and how much will go into each category or asset class. There are different ways to reach that goal of determining the right asset allocation for yourself. The basic approaches include:

**Doing it Yourself**
Selecting an investment mix from the investment options offered by your retirement account.

### Having it Done for You

Typically, this means a "target dated" fund, which has been selected for you based on your age and becomes increasingly more conservative as you grow older.

### Investment Analyzer

Using a comprehensive Investment Analyzer will guide you to a professionally managed model that reflects what is important about you and your financial situation. This will include your age, time to retirement, risk profile, and top two money personalities.

Here is an example of what different asset allocation models could look like.

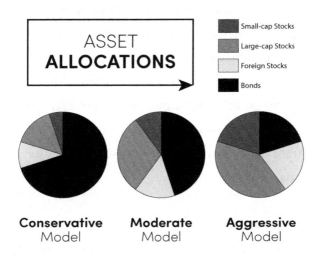

This example shows a conservative asset allocation model, a moderate asset allocation model, and an aggressive asset allocation model.

You will note that the difference between the three model allocations is the percentage of the total that is composed of stocks versus bonds—stocks typically being more aggressive and bonds being more conservative. So, an allocation of 50% stocks and 50% bonds would be a moderate allocation.

While the examples are simplified for illustration purposes, each category of investments can be more complex by adding different categories of either stocks or bonds. These categories are called asset classes.

During the 70s and early 80s, investment statisticians developed a very helpful method to help investors understand the relationship between risk and reward. It is called Modern Portfolio Theory. It plotted a graph that had risk on one axis and rate of return on the other.

Then a line was calculated that was called the Efficient Frontier. This Efficient Frontier line was drawn on the graph so that you could easily see where risk and reward meet.

Following is a chart illustrating the Efficient Frontier for a given investment. I am including this chart to make the point that there truly is a risk/reward relationship and that there can be a way to invest wisely over time. It is not just throwing darts at a board. That certainly is not good stewardship of God's resources.

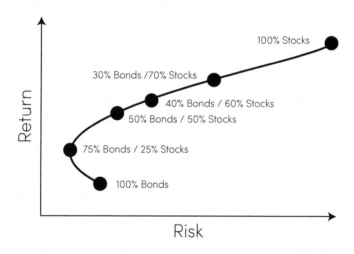

## Modern Portfolio Theory
Efficient Frontier

Since the early 80s, mutual funds have been the preferred vehicle to develop portfolios from the various asset classes. Mutual funds are professionally managed investment accounts that focus on specific types of investments. More recently a new way of managing money professionally has emerged: Exchange Traded Funds. While they are managed similarly to mutual funds, they are traded on the stock exchanges and are less costly. Look for ETFs to become the preferred investment type over the next number of years. This is primarily because of their reduced cost and similar rate of return to similar kinds of mutual funds.

## To Roth or Not?

One additional factor will impact your investment—should the contributions to your retirement account be pre-tax or after-tax? Pre-tax means that you don't pay taxes with every contribution, but you will pay taxes when you withdraw the money. On the other hand, the after-tax option, or Roth contribution, does not save taxes now but can if taken out tax free assuming the account has been in place for at least five years.

The Roth option is valuable and important to understand. Many in full-time ministry, or those on the lower end of the income spectrum, do not pay much income tax. We all complain about taxes, but you can make a mid to high 5 figure income with 3 children along with a commitment to tithing and be in a very low tax bracket.

One of the strong benefits of contributing to a retirement plan is the tax deductibility of your contribution. If you pay little income tax, that incentive goes away. A number of years ago, a congressman named Roth lead a campaign to create another tax incentive to save—no tax savings now, but no taxes to pay when you take the money out.

Interestingly, we sometimes pay more in taxes during retirement than during our earning years. That makes the Roth option very attractive. When you know that all or part of your Future Funded Ministry income will not be taxed, the incentive to save increases.

For most who pay little income tax, Roth is the way to go. Please discuss this option more with your tax advisor.

## Who Gets Your Money When You Die?

The individual or ministry who gets your remaining retirement account money when you die is called a beneficiary. If you do not designate a beneficiary, your account will be distributed according to state law and may not reflect what you want to happen. If you are married, your primary beneficiary will usually be your spouse, with children often being designated as secondary beneficiaries.

One very attractive option to deal with your retirement plan account as well as your other assets is to put a living trust in place. When you die, your estate will be distributed according to the laws of the state where you live. The court charged with overseeing that distribution is called the Probate Court. If you have a will, the will tells the Probate Court how you wish the assets to be distributed. The court appoints a probate attorney to help with this process. Depending on where you live, this process could take a long time and cost a lot of money.

The alternative to probate law is to create a living trust and a Trustee is appointed. Typically, the Trustee is you and your spouse while living, with a successor Trustee named by you in the event of your death or disability. The successor Trustee then has the power to distribute your assets according to your wishes reflected in the living trust.

The result is that your estate avoids Probate Court and results in a less costly and time-consuming process. While many attorneys and tax accountants only use the living trust process to try and save estate taxes, I maintain that setting up a living trust is the kindest and most loving thing you can do for yourself and your heirs. It keeps expenses down and simplifies the process. You may have heard of the nightmares families go through as the probate process unfolds.

If you have a living trust, your spouse will be your primary beneficiary, and the trust will be your secondary beneficiary. Consequently, if you and your spouse die at or around the same time, the terms of the trust will determine how your money is distributed. If you are single, you can name your trust as the primary beneficiary and have the money distributed according to the instruction in the trust document.

One last suggestion—rebalancing your account, taking it back to original percentages allocated or designated to each fund, reduces the overall risk of the portfolio. It makes sense to rebalance twice a year. Again, rebalancing means that the individual investments are rebalanced to the percentages originally designated.

The net result is that you are following the important investment adage of selling high and buying low. Here is how it works—when your account is rebalanced, the funds that have grown the most are sold, and the funds that have grown the least are purchased. Then your portfolio is rebalanced to its original percentages. It seems counter intuitive; however, the net result is that you are selling high and buying low. This is always a good idea.

Many retirement recordkeeping systems include a rebalancing feature that can be turned on or off by each plan participant. If your plan has such a feature, rebalancing every 6 months turns out to be the most advantageous time frame. Typically, there is no cost to take advantage of this feature.

# Questions & Application

Would you prefer to determine how your assets are allocated or have it distributed according to your age (target-dated):

_____

_____

_____

_____

Is an after-tax Roth contribution better for your current situation (why or why not):

_____

_____

_____

_____

What is the benefit to rebalancing your account:

_____

_____

_____

_____

# 13

## Now Is the Time

What will help encourage you as you put your Future Funded Ministry into motion? The answer—create a Vision Board. A vision is a picture you can see in your mind's eye. These pictures can inspire us, scare us, and motivate us, or they can direct us into hiding.

If you are married, it is important that you and your spouse contemplate and visualize your future. When you do, there is a greater likelihood that you will take action and prepare for that time of Future Funded Ministry.

Take a few minutes and begin visualizing your future. Collect photos, write down keywords, and make something tangible as a reminder you can change up. This can change the direction of your life starting now.

## Some Final Thoughts: A Postlude on Action and What's Next

Are you baffled, bewildered, or just plain stuck? You've stayed with us to the end. You are convinced that embracing the idea of "faithful for a lifetime" and that a Future Funded Ministry plan is imperative, but you can't seem to put your plan in motion. You are not alone.

My grandfather's words still ring in my ears, "Once begun is half done."

Here is a strange reality—most of us don't understand percentages. If asked, many retirement plan participants will say they cannot afford to contribute even 1% or 2%. Then, when I ask their salary, they say it is $48,000 per year and paid twice a month (24 times per year). If you divide $48,000 by 24, it equals $2,000 per pay period. So, 1% of $2,000 calculates to be $20 per pay period. They then look at me and say, "I can do that. As a matter of fact, make it $40 or 2%."

This small amount earning 6% for 20 years will produce about $300 per month at retirement. We went from "can't," to putting a savings plan into motion. Maybe the result won't cover all your needs, but it is certainly better than what is guaranteed if nothing had been done.

Just pick a spot and get started with your Vision Board. Or, just write down your income and your expenses. Start to get a picture of what is true now, while you visualize what can be. When all is said and done, if you don't put your Future Funded Ministry into motion, you will be stuck with nothing. We are each called and empowered to help build the Kingdom.

### *Now is the time and this is the place to put the funding of your future in MOTION!*

For many, connecting with the general and specific "call" on your life is cloudy. The whole idea may be new and somewhat perplexing. This is the call extended to you by God the Father to represent Jesus to the world while being empowered by the Holy Spirit to accomplish building his Kingdom here on earth. As a pastor friend of mine proclaims, "Stepping with faith into your preferred future." I like that.

Our first book, Finding Freedom, may help and I encourage you to read it as a resource and for clarity. Hopefully the process and perspective of putting your Future Funded Ministry into motion, the book you've just read, is encouraging as well. Rest assured that the next book about how you can hear God's call on your life will be life changing.

You are chosen to build the kingdom and are called to a specific role in that construction process. You are strengthened by God to fulfill the call and will be encouraged by the Holy Spirit when the going gets rough. God cares, God prepares, and God communicates with those who are open to listening. In the upcoming book, we will help you to listen for His call and respond to it. That response will change your life and even change the world.

Many 50 and 60-year old's view retirement, that 4th quarter, as a time of diminished importance. Nothing could be further from the truth! We are called to a life of meaning and purpose—for a lifetime, not just for a season. Those approaching that life stage will want to read the next book and then pass it on to a friend.

Bruce Bruinsma

## Take the next step ...

Visit brucebruinsma.com/moving-forward-resources online for additional tools, resources, and information to help you move forward.

# Questions & Application

Describe a few things you would like to do during retirement, and if this is now different from before reading this book:

_____

_____

_____

_____

What are three things you need to make sure your future ministry is funded:

_____

_____

_____

_____

How has the information in this book helped you:

_____

_____

_____

_____

## About Bruce Bruinsma

Bruce is the Founder of Envoy Financial and the Live with Meaning Foundation, which inspire and empower people for a lifetime of ministry. In addition, he is the co-creator of several businesses that financially support ministries and communities in the United States, Europe, and Asia.

Bruce holds an MBA from the University of California, Berkeley and has more than 40 years of professional experience in retirement planning and finance. He is the authors of three books, consults with Christian ministries worldwide, and is a sought-after presenter. Currently, he lives in Colorado with his wife Judy.

For more information, go to BruceBruinsma.com

## The Retirement Reformation

Our calling to love and serve others doesn't end at retirement. In fact, retirement could be the season of your life where you have the greatest impact for God's Kingdom. You have unique passions, abilities, and experiences that God wants to use in ALL seasons and stages of your life.

Discover your calling. Maximize your life. Change your world. Join the Retirement Reformation at RetirementReformation.org.

# Appendix

**Book Questions**

- What could you see yourself doing during the ACTIVE APPLICATION stage of retirement?

- What could you see yourself doing during the INSIGHTFUL STEWARDSHIP stage of retirement?

- What could you see yourself doing during the REFLECTIVE SHARING stage of retirement?

- Have you ever considered preparing for retirement as a funding a future ministry (if not, explain why)?

- Do you agree with the concept of a future funded ministry (explain your answer below)?

- If more Christians embraced a future funded ministry, do you think it would change anything?

- Why is it important to understand your current and future life stages?

- If you are a pastor, minister, or missionary, what are some unique financial advantages available to you?

- When is the best time to start preparing financially?

- Since retirement is a long way away, do you think it is important to start saving now (why or why not)?

- What are some good first steps to take during this life stage?

- Once you start saving for the future, what should you resist doing?

- If you have not started saving for retirement, is it too late?

- How can children affect your financial planning and preparation?

- What are some options for investing extra

income once you have maxed out your retirement plan?

- How do (or could) you feel about your financial approach to retirement during this life stage?

- What contribution advantage do you have once you have passed age 50?

- Is it too late to consider supplemental income after 50?

- What are some advantages of your Money Personalities?

- What are some disadvantages of your Money Personalities?

- How can understanding your Money Personalities and those of others affect your relationship with your spouse, kids, and others?

- What are a few terms that you have heard before but never understood until reading this book?

- Is it important for someone to understand these basic terms (why or why not)?

- What is your risk tolerance, and why is it important to know what it is?

- Would you prefer to determine how your assets are allocated or have it distributed according to your age (target-dated)?

- Is an after-tax Roth contribution better for your current situation (why or why not)?

- What is the benefit to rebalancing your account?

- Describe a few things you would like to do during retirement, and if this is now different from before reading this book?

- What are three things you need to make sure your future ministry is funded?

- How has the information in this book helped you?

# References

Lake, Rebecca. (2018, October 10). *Average Retirement Savings by Age.* Retrieved from https://www.thebalance.com/average-retirement-savings-by-age-4155888

Employee Benefit Research Institute. (2010, July). *Retirement Income Preparation and Future Prospects.* Retrieved from https://www.ebri.org/publications/ib/index.cfm?fa=ibDisp&content_id=4593

Fidelity Investments. (2016, August 16). *Health Care Costs for Couples in Retirement Rise to an Estimated $260,000, Fidelity Analysis Shows.* Retrieved from https://www.fidelity.com/about-fidelity/employer-services/health-care-costs-for-couples-in-retirement-rise

Made in the USA
Middletown, DE
02 October 2023

39957708R00096